TALLER TALES
with Mr. K

Kathy Sattem Rygg

Made Possible by an
Anonymous Donation
2019

Text copyright 2017 by Kathy Sattem Rygg
Cover Illustration copyright 2017

All rights reserved. Published by knowonder! publishing. knowonder!, knowonder! magazine, and associated logos, are trademarks and/or registered trademarks of knowonder! publishing.

No part of this publication may be reproduced, either in part or in whole, or stored in an electronic or retrieval system, or transmitted in any form or by any means, including electronic, mechanical, photocopying, recording, or otherwise, without the express written permission of the publisher. For information regarding permission, contact knowonder via email: editor@knowonder.com

Taller Tales with Mr. K / DyslexiAssist Enabled / Kathy Sattem Rygg

ISBN: 978-1-5427434-0-2

1. Fiction 2. Fantasy 3. Early Reader Chapter Book

Printed in the U.S.A.
First Edition, 2017

for Jack
and Peter

About DyslexiAssist

Part of our mission at *Knowonder! Publishing* is to make literacy more effective. In order to fulfill that mission we are proud to announce our new DyslexiAssist initiative: to publish books in a special font and layout designed to make reading easier for children suffering from dyslexia.

When reading with this new font, independent research shows that 84% of dyslexics read faster, 77% read with fewer mistakes, and 76% recommend the font to others who suffer from dyslexia.

But the magic isn't just in the font. We take extra care to make the font an appropriate size, give proper spacing to letters in the words, make sure that there are the exact right number of words on each line, and so much more! The layout of the book is critical. In fact, recent peer-reviewed scientific research showed that all the dyslexic children read easier and faster with the proper increased spacing.[1] What amazing news!

And so, we here at Knowonder go to extra lengths to make sure all the stars are aligned so all children know the wonder of reading.

We hope this new initiative can now bring a new and increased love and joy of reading and learning to your home!

> Learn more, including how you can use DyslexiAssist in your home or classroom for FREE at knowonder.com/dyslexiassist

email us at phillip@knowonder.com and we'll send you a copy of the study.

1. THE MYSTERIOUS MR. K – WE MEET AGAIN

Eli raced down the stairs, rounded the corner in his living room, and skidded across the wood kitchen floor, grabbing his brown lunch bag waiting for him on the counter.

"You're going to be late." His mother stood by the back door with her arms folded in front of her chest.

"I'm going!" Eli shoved his feet into his new black and neon yellow Nikes. He threw his backpack over one shoulder, patted his grey and white Husky on the head, and sprinted out the door.

"Have a good day," his mom called after him. He waved without turning around.

His feet pounded the sidewalk, and he worked up a light sweat despite the chill in the morning air. One of his shoelaces came untied, the plastic end tapping against the sidewalk with each stride. He didn't have time to stop and re-tie it and risk being late for his first day of third grade.

By the time he reached the school's main doors,

his chest heaved with each gasping breath. He spotted his best friend's red Cardinals backpack and joined his group of classmates.

"Hey, Woody, did the bell ring yet?" Eli asked, bending over to catch his breath.

"Nope. You're here just in time." Woody slapped him on the back as Eli let out a sigh of relief.

"I was afraid I was going to miss the big entrance. After hearing all the rumors, I can't wait to see it with my own eyes." Eli grinned.

"Rumors about what?" A long, leggy boy who looked like a string bean peered around Woody.

"Not 'what,' more like 'who,'" Woody said. "The rumors about Mr. K."

The string bean shrugged. "Who's Mr. K?"

Woody's jaw dropped. "You haven't heard about Mr. K? Where have you been living, Siberia?"

"I just transferred to Coyote Run from a different school."

"Mr. K is only the greatest teacher in the whole history of teachers," Woody said.

"He's also the tallest teacher in the history of teachers," Eli added.

"Don't forget the baldest." Whitney DeWulf, who had been chatting with a group of girls, turned around and chimed in. "And, according to my older sister Karly's diary, he's magical, too," she added.

The string bean frowned. "Our third grade teacher

is magical? Doubtful."

"It's true!" Woody said. "Everything about him is out of the ordinary. Instead of desks his students get to sit at picnic tables, and apple trees grow all around the room."

"Yeah, and there's a giant traffic light hanging from the ceiling that buzzes so loud when the light turns red, your eardrums literally burst," Eli said.

"Just wait. You'll see it all when we walk in the classroom. I've been waiting all summer for this." Woody reached up and gave Eli a high five.

The school bell rang, and Eli followed the herd of students shuffling through the front doors. A rush of chatter filled the halls—except the one leading to

Mr. K's classroom. The third graders fell silent as they approached. Then they burst inside.

Within seconds, their excited expressions fell from their faces, replaced by scowls and confusing glances.

"Are we in the right room?" Eli asked, staring at the ordinary desks and chairs.

Not a single apple tree lined the walls. Instead, a fake plant in a basket was shoved in one corner. The only thing hanging from the ceiling was a screen projector. And sitting behind the teacher's desk was Mr. K—although he didn't look that tall.

"Everyone find your assigned seats," Mr. K said in a gentle voice.

Woody and Eli exchanged glances as the students

zigzagged around the room, looking for their name cards on top of each desk.

Eli's desk was toward the back of the room in between Woody and the string bean.

"This is a total rip-off," Woody muttered. He slumped in his chair and crossed his arms in front of his chest.

The bean had an "I-told-you-so" smirk on his face. Eli sighed and arranged his school supplies in the storage cubby underneath his desk. Maybe the new kid was right—Mr. K wasn't magical after all.

The final bell rang, and Mr. K took attendance. "Andrew Allen?"

"Here." A red-headed boy stuck his arm in the

air.

"Sage Gregarian?" Mr. K glanced around the room.

"Here." A stocky girl with a boy's haircut nodded.

"Gregarian? More like barbarian." Woody reached over and nudged Eli on the elbow, snickering. "Grayson Howell?" Mr. K said.

The bean raised his arm in the air and nodded.

"Yes sir. Present."

Woody rolled his eyes at Eli.

Mr. K continued with roll call, finally reaching the end of the alphabet. "James Woodbury?"

"Just call me Woody. Everyone else does."

Mr. K studied him for a minute and then smiled a friendly half-smile.

He didn't waste any time launching into work. Even though it was the first day of school, Mr. K had them solve math equations, practice spelling words, and study the Constitution.

Eli's head drooped lower with each passing hour, and his spirit deflated. First, they walk into an ordinary classroom, and then Mr. K doesn't do anything special. The only thing worse would be if someone canceled Christmas.

"Class, please open your guided reading books to chapter one," Mr. K said when they came back after lunch. The ruffling of turning pages filled the silent classroom. Eli didn't even bother to groan, which was his normal reaction to doing a reading assignment.

Mr. K glanced around the room and then slammed his book closed. "All right. Either something is bothering you, or aliens have invaded and taken over your bodies. This is the saddest group of third graders I've ever seen on the first day of school."

Eli picked at a corner of his book cover. Several students squirmed in their seats.

"Come on, now," Mr. K said. "If you don't tell me what's wrong, we can't fix it."

Whitney raised her hand and Mr. K nodded at her. "Well...it's just that...we thought the classroom would be...you know, special."

Mr. K's eyebrows shot up in surprise. "Special? How?"

"We thought it'd be like last year," Whitney continued. "With picnic tables, apple trees, and the traffic light."

"Yeah, and I've been chewing this same piece of gum all day hoping to add it to the giant gum wad," said Randy Hester. "But you haven't even noticed, and my jaw feels like it's about to fall off."

"Is this how you all feel?" Mr. K asked.

Eli mumbled "yes" and nodded along with the rest of his classmates.

"I'm sorry to disappoint you, but I'm afraid I had to give up all those items once last year's class graduated to fourth grade." Mr. K rubbed the top of his shiny head. "Tell you what. I'll make it up to you by giving you an extra recess. We'll read one chapter from our book then you can head back outside."

"Sounds like a good deal to me," Grayson said.

Woody glared at him. "You wouldn't know a good deal if it snapped your skinny body right in half."

Just like a string bean. Eli snickered at the thought. It was the first time he had smiled all day.

The students perked up a little during their extra recess, but a group of them gathered on the blacktop to discuss Mr. K and his lack of...mystery.

"Do you think last year's class just made the whole thing up?" Eli asked.

Whitney adjusted the purple sequined headband in her dark, wavy hair. "Trust me, my sister Karly could never make up a story like that. She's not that bright."

"I know, we could rise up and protest, just like they did during the Resolutionary War," Woody said.

"Revolutionary War," Whitney corrected him.

"Whatever, Webster. My point is, we can refuse to do any work until Mr. K does something cool for us."

"We could make signs," Eli said. "They'd say, 'No School 'Til Something Cool.'"

"That's awesome!" Woody gave him a fist bump. "As soon as we get back inside, everyone make a sign in their notebooks, and when Mr. K starts class, we'll hold them up. No school 'til something cool!"

"No school 'til something cool!" several students yelled back.

The playground teacher blew the whistle, and the entire third-grade chanted their new slogan on the way inside. But they fell silent as they approached their classroom door. Then they marched inside.

Within seconds, their excited expressions fell from their faces, replaced by gasps and jaw-dropping shock.

The regular desks and chairs in the classroom had been replaced by rows of airplane seats— complete with drop-down tray tables and running lights in the aisles. The fake potted plant in the corner was dwarfed by a clump of corn stalks, their silky tops almost touching the ceiling. A giant JumboTron TV and scoreboard hung in the middle of the room, just like at a sports arena. And towering over the tiny teacher's desk stood Mr. K, his completely bald head (well, mostly bald) reflecting the room's bright fluorescent lights.

"Is this cool enough for you?" Mr. K asked.

Woody and Eli grinned at each other. "Awesome," Eli whispered.

He and Woody claimed seats next to each other. They opened and closed their tray tables and tested their seatbacks to see if they reclined—they did.

"Why are there barf bags in the seat pockets?" Grayson asked.

"That's in case you get a bad grade on a test," Whitney said. Grayson gave her a confused look. "According to my sister's diary, if you get a 'D' Mr. K makes you eat duck liver. And if you get an 'F' he makes you eat foot fungus."

Grayson grimaced and slowly slid the white paper bag back into the seat pocket.

Eli studied the JumboTron overhead. The scoreboard listed two teams. Mr. K's name was one and "Class" was the other. He raised his hand. "Mr. K, what's the deal with the JumboTron?"

"I'm going to keep score," Mr. K said. "Every

time the class is quiet, finishes your work on time, or someone helps out another student, you get a point." He pushed a button on a remote control on his desk and the number "1" flashed on the scoreboard. "But any time you are noisy or someone misbehaves, I get a point." He clicked another button and a flashing number "1" appeared underneath his name on the scoreboard. "When the class reaches ten points, you'll get to watch a movie on the big screen and enjoy popcorn—made fresh from the corn picked right off our stalks."

"What happens if you reach ten points first?" Randy asked.

"Instead of eating popcorn, you'll have to take a

pop quiz. Which means if you haven't studied for it, you may not receive a very high grade. And I have a feeling you already know what happens then."

Whitney turned around in her seat and pointed to Grayson's seat pocket. "Barf bag time." Grayson's face turned as white as his bag. Mr. K opened one of his desk drawers and pulled out a bright green box. "Everyone please put down your tray tables." He walked down the first aisle of airplane seats and placed a round object on each tray table.

Eli picked his up. It looked like a giant orange gumball. He sniffed it and then gave it a lick. It tasted like candy, too.

"I want everyone to spend the next five minutes

chewing up their gumball," Mr. K said. "I gave my old gum wad to a former student, so we need to make a new one."

The students popped the gumballs into their mouths and chewed, and chewed, and chewed. After five minutes Mr. K walked back down the aisles, collecting the pieces of ABC—already been chewed—gum and smashing them into a rainbow-colored ball of sticky, mushy goo.

"You know the rule," he said. "The first time you chew gum in my class you add to the wad. The next time I catch you chewing gum, what happens to the wad?"

"You have to eat it!" the class yelled.

"Now that we have all that out of the way, let's get down to work." Mr. K sat back down at his desk, his knees sticking out on either side.

Eli flipped down his tray table, ready for whatever Mr. K had for them. The changes to the room were even better than what he had hoped for.

Woody pushed on Grayson's seat in front of him. "See, I told you he was the best teacher in the world."

Grayson peered back at him from in between the seats. "So, it doesn't make him magical."

"Oh yeah? Then how do you explain the room?" Woody said.

"He could easily have had a whole crew bring this

stuff in here while we were at recess. So far, I don't see anything magical about him."

Woody snickered. "Just wait."

2. THE SPECTACULAR SPY

One month into the new school year things were looking good in Mr. K's classroom. The students had finally earned enough points to have their first popcorn party, complete with a movie on the JumboTron.

Woody squirmed in his seat, squinting at the screen. Something about it didn't seem right; it was like sitting in the front row at a movie theater.

"What are you doing?" Eli asked. "Why do you keep scrunching up your nose like that?"

"Does the movie seem out of focus to you?" Woody asked.

"No. It's just you. You probably need glasses or something."

"Yeah, right. I wouldn't be caught dead in glasses." Woody scribbled in his notebook, refusing to look at the screen again. The blurry picture was giving him a headache.

Afterward, Mr. K approached Woody's seat. "I couldn't help but notice you didn't seem interested in the movie. Don't you like movies about giant peaches?"

"It's because he couldn't see it very well," Eli said. Woody gave him a dirty look.

"Aha. I think we better take a walk down to the nurse's office. Class, please start on your independent reading until I get back." Mr. K led Woody by the shoulders out of the classroom to Mrs. Huerter's office, the school nurse.

Woody scowled and stared at Mrs. Heurter's short, spiked black hair and cotton candy pink lipstick. He tried faking his way through the eye exam but didn't get past the giant letter 'E' at the top of the chart.

"There's no doubt about it, James, you need glasses," Mrs. Heurter said.

Woody's head rolled back and his mouth dropped open. He couldn't think of anything worse than having to get glasses. Everyone would make fun of him.

"I'll send a note home to your parents letting them know you need to see an eye doctor."

Mr. K thanked her and led Woody out of the office. "That wasn't so bad," he said.

Woody glanced up—all the way up—at Mr. K.

"Easy for you to say. You don't wear glasses. My brother has them, and they're always getting lost or broken. It's a huge pain." Not to mention people calling his brother "four-eyes."

"But they also help you see things in a way nobody else can."

"How?"

"Come with me. I'll show you." Mr. K turned the corner and led Woody down another hall. He stopped in front of a wooden door with a sign beside it that read, "TEACHER'S LOUNGE."

Woody had no idea what was in the boring teacher's lounge that could help make him feel any better about having to get glasses.

Mr. K opened the door. Woody followed him inside...or rather, outside. They stood on the roof of a building behind a short wall that overlooked a busy city street below. Red brake lights from cars blazed in the evening light as people hurried up and down the busy sidewalk. The aromas of grilled burgers and fries from nearby restaurants clung to the warm air, and music played somewhere in the distance.

Woody backed away from the building's guard rail, his stomach pulsating from being up so high. He looked at Mr. K and gasped when he noticed his teacher's usual khaki pants and white golf shirt had been replaced by black cargo pants, a black T-shirt, and a black bag strapped across his chest.

"What are we doing on top of a building in the middle of Main Street? And why are you dressed like a ninja?" Woody looked down and noticed he was wearing all black, too.

"Agent Woodbury, you've been chosen for a top-secret mission. In five minutes, a woman is going to walk out of that dry cleaners down there, carrying a special package. She's going to walk down the street and head into the park where she's going to drop the package somewhere. You need to follow her and intercept the package before the other party gets to it."

Woody scoffed. "You want me to be a spy?"

"We prefer to call them special agents. Are you up for the mission?"

Woody glanced at the street below. "But there's tons of people around. And the park is pitch black at night. How am I supposed to keep track of her? I don't see very well, remember?"

"That's why I brought you these." Mr. K reached

into his black bag and pulled out a pair of glasses with sleek black rims. He placed them over Woody's eyes.

A big grin erupted across Woody's face. "Whoa! These are amazing! I can see in the dark. Everything is bright...and kind of greenish colored." He looked at the street below. "I can see everybody. I can even see that cat in the alleyway."

"Good. Now take the elevator inside the building down to the ground floor. Go across the street and stand in front of the book store. I'll signal from up here when the woman comes out."

Woody did as Mr. K instructed, his heart thumping inside his chest from nerves and excitement.

He walked across the street to the bookstore and stood in front of the window. Even from down here, he could clearly see Mr. K standing on top of the building.

A bell jingled above the drycleaner's door when it opened, and a woman wearing a long dark trench coat hurried out, carrying a silver briefcase. She turned away from where Woody stood so he only caught a glimpse of her from the back. He noticed she had short, spiked dark hair—just like Nurse Huerter.

He glanced up at Mr. K who made a fist. That was the signal, so this must be the woman. Woody scurried down the sidewalk, weaving around a constant flood of people walking in both directions.

The woman's coat billowed around her legs, and she disappeared in the crowd for seconds at a time. Woody jogged to keep up, focusing his gaze on her coat and hair.

At the end of Main Street, she turned the corner and crossed into the park. Woody followed, the noise and traffic fading behind him. He maintained a greater distance once on the park's bike path, which seemed deserted compared to downtown. A few late-night joggers ran by, and several couples strolled hand-in-hand. The woman never turned around or glanced in any direction. She kept her head facing forward and moved with a steady stride.

It was much darker in the park, with only a few

lampposts providing pools of light on the path.

Woody's glasses gave him a clear view of her movements. He was dying to know if she could possibly be the school nurse. If he could just get a glimpse of her face, he'd know as soon as he saw if she wore bright pink lipstick or not.

The woman reached the center of the park and slowed down by the giant stone fountain. Woody ducked behind a tree, peering around its thick trunk. The woman set the silver briefcase down underneath a park bench and then continued down the bike path into the dark.

Woody stepped out from behind the tree, waiting to make sure she didn't return. He started toward the briefcase when he noticed a man appear around the fountain, heading straight for the park bench. It had to be the enemy. Woody needed to get to that briefcase first!

He took a deep breath and then broke out into a run. The man must have seen Woody because he sprinted toward the briefcase, reaching it just seconds before Woody. Then he dashed away from the fountain and through the trees.

Woody chased after him, following the man's clear outline that the special night-vision glasses provided. He ran full-speed, darting around trees and gaining on the man. He couldn't let him get away— Mr. K was counting on him.

They approached the entrance at the opposite end of the park. If the man ran back into the crowded street, Woody might lose him. This was his only chance. With a final burst of speed, he caught up to the man, only inches away. Woody reached out, grabbed the back of the man's coat collar, and pulled. The coat slid off the man's back, but his arm that held onto the briefcase caught in the sleeve. The man switched the briefcase to his other hand and shimmied out of the coat.

"What? No!" Woody yelled. The man was about to get away. Woody had no choice. He put his head down, pumped his arms, and leaped into the air, landing on the man's back and tackling him to the ground. His glasses flew off, but Woody grabbed the briefcase with both hands and held on. The man stood up and tried to run. Woody heard a crunching sound on the ground as the man dragged him for several feet.

"I'm not letting go," Woody said through clenched teeth.

Shouts and voices came from behind. The man looked up, startled, and then let go of the briefcase and disappeared across the street into the crowd.

Woody rolled over onto his back, clutching the briefcase to his chest and trying to catch his breath. When he looked up, he saw Mr. K standing over him.

"Nice work, Agent Woodbury." Mr. K reached

down and helped Woody off the ground. "You never let the package out of your sight." He took the briefcase from Woody.

"The glasses made it easy," Woody said. "But they fell off, and I think the guy stepped on them."

"Not to worry," said Mr. K. "You completed your mission. It's time to go back."

"Already? I could get used to this spy stuff." Woody followed Mr. K to the park entrance. They walked out of the park and back into—the hallway at school!

Woody blinked several times, adjusting his eyes to the bright indoor lights after having been in the dark park. "Whoa, how did you do that?"

"Just one of the perks of being a third-grade teacher," Mr. K said. "Ready to head back to class?"

"I guess." Woody nodded toward the briefcase in Mr. K's hand. "What's in there that's so important?"

Mr. K held the small case level and then clicked open the locks. The lid flipped up, revealing a pair of dark-rimmed eye glasses. "The package is for you."

Woody grinned, carefully picked up the glasses, and placed them on his face. "They look just like the other ones. Will I be able to see at night with these?"

"I have a feeling you'll be able to see everything in a whole new light," Mr. K said, and then smiled a half-smile.

3. THE GAME SHOW GENIUS

As the third graders grew anxious for fall break, they seemed to forget all the rules of the classroom, resulting in their first pop quiz of the year. Mr. K handed out a worksheet filled with math, science, and social studies questions they had never seen before.

"Oh, man, this is gonna be bad." Woody removed his glasses and rubbed his eyes. "I might as well get my barf bag out right now."

"These are easy," Whitney said in a cheerful voice. "Everybody knows the body of water on the west coast of Florida is the Gulf of Mexico."

"I didn't," Woody said. "At least I'll get one right now. Hey, what planets are closest to Earth?"

Whitney glared at him. "Like I'd tell you. Do your own work." She snapped her head back and bent low over her paper.

Woody scowled. "You're such a know-it-all, Webster. It gets really old, not to mention annoying. You make all of us look bad. No wonder why you don't have any friends."

Whitney didn't dare look back at him. She wasn't about to give him the satisfaction of seeing tears in her eyes.

After the quiz, a college-aged man with swooping hair across his forehead strode into the classroom.

"Whitney, Mr. Garrett needs to meet with you early today," Mr. K said.

Grayson leaned over to Randy, who sat next to him. "Who's Mr. Garrett?"

"He's the teacher who works with the smart kids," Randy said.

Grayson folded his arms on his chest. "I'm smart. How come I've never met with him?"

Randy shrugged. "Because you're not Whitney DeWulf smart."

Whitney sat frozen in her airplane seat. She

didn't want to meet with Mr. Garrett today. She didn't want to meet with him again ever. She wanted to be normal, like all the other kids.

"Whitney, is there a problem?" Mr. K asked. 33

She bit her lip to keep it from trembling.

Mr. K regarded her for a minute and then turned to Mr. Garrett. "I'll bring her down in a little while, if that's okay with you?"

"No problem-o," Mr. Garrett said, flashing a bright white grin.

"Class, please read independently. Whitney, come with me." Mr. K stood up, ducking as he walked underneath the JumboTron, and walked into the hall. Whitney slid out of her seat and followed, assuming

Mr. K was escorting her to Mr. Garrett's classroom.

But Mr. K walked right past it, not stopping until he reached the door to the teacher's lounge. Whitney's eyes bulged. This was just like what her sister wrote in her diary. Was she about to walk through the door into a trapeze act at the circus? But she was afraid of heights!

Mr. K placed his hand on the doorknob and then stopped and addressed her. "I know intelligence isn't always appreciated by your classmates. But I think after this, they'll have a different opinion." He turned the silver handle with a click and walked through the door.

Whitney followed Mr. K, marching behind him into

the middle of the room. But it wasn't a room. It was a stage! Bright lights flashed on overhead. Quirky music blared from giant speakers off-stage. Cheers erupted from the audience, which was filled with kids. Whitney's mouth hung open as she glanced at the glittery podium off to the side and rainbow-striped curtain that hung behind her. It all seemed oddly familiar to her.

A smiling man dressed in purple plaid shorts and a lime green shirt strode toward her with a small headset sticking out behind his ear. His face was a strange peach color, like he had on too much makeup. His long bangs swooped over his forehead—just like Mr. Garrett's.

"Ladies and germs, welcome to everyone's favorite game show, 'Brain Warriors'! I'm your host, Skip Hoppe. Our first contestant today is one smart cookie. Let's give a warm welcome to Whitney DeWulf!"

"What?" Whitney spun around, staring at Mr. K. How could she be on "Brain Warriors"? It was one of the most popular kid game shows on TV. She and her sister watched it every day after school. Contestants had to answer random questions. If they got them all correct they had a chance at making it through the Craze Maze in thirty seconds.

The maze was filled with impossible hazards, like whipped cream covered balance beams, insect-filled pools, and the Knowledge Ninjas—stealthy brainiacs who appeared out of nowhere and peppered the contestant with questions that had to be answered in nanoseconds. If the contestant won, they became a Mind Master and got prizes worth thousands of dollars.

Nobody had ever won.

"Good luck. You'll be great!" Mr. K gave her a thumbs-up and then jogged off to the side of the stage, leaving Whitney alone with the grinning Skip.

"Come on over to the cranium podium." Skip motioned for Whitney to follow. She stepped onto a short stool behind the podium, which had a microphone bent over the top.

"Tell us, Whitney, where do you go to school?" Skip asked.

"Coyote Run Elementary." Her voice boomed throughout the studio.

"Coyote Run? What do we say to that, audience?" A chorus of howls broke out on set.

Whitney's cheeks felt warm from her embarrassment. "Are you ready to play 'Brain Warriors'?"

Whitney took a deep breath and nodded. "Then let's get started!"

A giant screen descended from the ceiling. "Whitney, here is your first question. Why does your grandmother have wrinkles?" The question appeared on the screen above a photo of an elderly woman—but not Whitney's grandmother.

Whitney gave Skip a confused look. Was this a trick question? She was about to say it was because her grandmother was old, but then she realized it was a trick question. Why did old people's skin wrinkle? Her mom always slathered lotion on her face "to keep it stretchy." She leaned over toward the microphone.

"My grandmother has wrinkles because her skin isn't stretchy anymore."

Skip hesitated. "That's...correct!" The audience whooped. Whitney looked at Mr. K and smiled.

"Here is your next question. Why do the bottoms of your hands and feet wrinkle in water?" Whitney's stomach balled up. Another wrinkle question? It couldn't be the same answer as the first. She stared at her palms. If they wrinkled in water, it must be because water gets under her skin. She blurted out the first answer that made sense. "Because they're not waterproof?"

The studio fell silent. "You are...correct-a-mundo!" Skip bellowed. The audience cheered.

Whitney's confidence grew. This wasn't so bad.

"Final question, Whitney. Why does this dog have wrinkles?" A photo of a tan dog with a smushed face and rolls of furry wrinkles appeared on the giant screen.

Whitney knew the dog was a Shar-pei. Her

neighbor, Mrs. Rosencrantz, owned a Shar-pei named Rolly. One time Rolly got loose and wound up in a fight with Fritz, another neighbor's German Shepherd. Rolly didn't get hurt, and Mrs. Rosencrantz said it was because all those wrinkles protected him. Whitney didn't know if she was right, but it was worth a shot.

"That dog has wrinkles to protect him from getting hurt." She held her breath.

Skip put his finger to his ear, as though listening to something. "What do the judges say?" Several seconds passed. "They say...okay! You are correct!" The audience leapt to their feet and hollered. Then they started chanting "Craze maze, Craze Maze,

Craze Maze."

"Whitney, it looks like you get thirty seconds in the Craze Maze!" The rainbow-colored curtain opened, revealing a giant system of clear plastic tubes, platforms, and walls. Skip handed her a helmet and safety goggles. Her stomach flipped and her heart raced as she put on the equipment. Answering questions was one thing; the Craze Maze was a challenge she wasn't ready for.

"Okay, Whitney, your thirty seconds begins when the green light comes on. Ready, set, go!"

As soon as Whitney saw a green flash out of the corner of her eye she crawled into the first tube. It started to spin, throwing her off balance as she tumbled against the sides. She kept on her hands and knees and scurried to the end of the tube, which opened above a large blow-up pool filled with something black— insects.

She jumped down and closed her eyes as she immersed herself waist-deep in the bugs. Her shoes made crunching sounds when she landed. She opened her eyes and squealed—cockroaches! The insects scuttled up her arms and legs, and Whitney swallowed back the urge to vomit.

Just get to the other side, she told herself, and then waded through the sea of black bugs.

Hanging above the other side of the pool was a rope ladder. Whitney climbed up to the top, ignoring the burning sensation on her palms. A long, narrow platform covered in a white gooey substance waited for her—the whipped cream balance beam. This was the trickiest part. If you fell off, you lost. There was no way to get back up and finish the Craze Maze.

Whitney placed her feet on the end of the beam and inched her way out. The whipped cream had started to melt, turning the bottom of her Mary Jane shoes into ice skates. She'd have to take her time. She glanced at the huge digital clock in front of her—only fifteen seconds left—she didn't have time!

She slid her feet along the platform faster and almost reached the other side when her right foot slipped on the edge. Whitney teetered, leaning forward and backward, her arms pin wheeling in the air. The audience gasped, but she regained her balance, and with a final step, made it safely to the other side.

Without hesitating, she ducked into the top of the next tube and slid down. It dumped her out onto a heaping pile of spongy cubes. She scrambled through them toward the final obstacle, a plastic-walled maze. She started to wind her way through it when someone dressed all in black sprang in front of her—a Knowledge Ninja!

"What is the capitol of Peru?" the ninja rattled. Whitney's head spun. She knew this. It had something to do with beans... "Lima!"

The ninja disappeared, and Whitney ran around the corner, almost smacking into another black-clad person.

"What is the square root of 144?" the ninja fired off.

Whitney knew this one. "It's twelve!"

The ninja jumped out of the way, and Whitney whipped around the wall, spotting the end of the maze and the finish line. Suddenly, a third ninja stepped in front of her.

"How many players are on the field during a football game?"

Whitney froze. Football? She didn't know much about sports. Her dad watched football on TV all the time. She tried picturing the formation in her mind. The audience started counting down from ten—her time was almost up! Then she remembered something—the boys at school played football during recess. She had heard them say how many were on each team.

"Three, two..." the audience chanted.

She remembered! "Twenty-two players!" The ninja stepped aside and Whitney dove across the finish line just as the buzzer sounded. The audience leapt to their feet, cheering wildly.

Skip ran over to Whitney and helped her up.

"You did it! You won! You're our first Mind Master!" He held her arm in the air. "Tell her what's she's won." A voice over the speakers rattled off a list of prizes, but Whitney only caught part of it amid the roars and claps from the audience.

After several minutes, Skip escorted Whitney off-stage where Mr. K was waiting.

"So, how does it feel to be a Mind Master?" he asked.

Whitney beamed. "Amazing!" Her head was still dizzy with excitement. She followed him back stage and out a side door—right into the hallway outside their classroom at school. When she walked into the room, the entire third-grade class turned around in their seats and cheered as she entered. Whitney looked around, embarrassed and confused.

"I can't believe you were a contestant on 'Brain Warriors'!" Sage said. "Why didn't you tell us?"

Whitney glanced at Mr. K. "The class watched the show on the JumboTron," he said.

"They did?" Whitney's stomach dropped.

"You were awesome!" Woody said. "I'd never be able to beat the ninjas. You're lucky you're so smart."

"Thanks." Whitney's heart soared from her classmates' praise.

"So what did you win?" Woody asked.

"A bunch of prizes."

Woody gave her a disappointed look. "There is one really cool prize, though. I get twenty free passes to see a live taping of the show, and I thought it might be fun for our whole class to go. You know, like a field trip."

"Yes!" Woody jumped up, and the class chattered with excitement.

"Would that be okay, Mr. K?" Whitney asked.

"No problem-o," Mr. K said, and then smiled his half-smile.

4. THE AWE-INSPIRED ASTRONAUT

The third graders had been having such a blast in Mr. K's class first semester, they couldn't believe winter break had arrived. It also meant it was time for the class holiday party. The school's Parent Teacher Organization planned games and provided treats for all the students.

After two rounds of holiday Bingo and a contest

to see who could come up with the funniest lyrics to the tune "Jingle Bells," Mr. K handed out juice pouches and frosted cookies to the students.

Randy wrinkled his nose as Mr. K set a round cookie in front of him with blue frosting and iridescent sprinkles on top that looked like snowflakes.

"Don't worry, Randy," Mr. K said. "The PTO ordered these cookies from a local bakery that doesn't use any peanut products, so your allergies won't be a problem."

"I bet they're not gluten-free though," Randy mumbled.

"You have an issue with food that contains

gluten, too? When did that come up?"

Randy rested his head in his hand. "I was just tested this week. It's bad enough I have to sit at the peanut-free table by myself every day at lunch. Now I can't eat anything good anymore, either. Nothing with wheat products, which means no cookies, cereal, or even mac n' cheese. Can you believe that? Not even lousy mac n' cheese."

Mr. K gave Randy a sympathetic look. "Lots of people can't eat gluten these days, and the grocery stores are full of gluten-free food choices. I've even seen gluten-free mac n' cheese."

"Yeah, but it tastes like cardboard." Randy handed the cookie back to Mr. K and folded up his tray table. "I hate not being able to eat what everyone else can eat. Just once I'd like to sit at the hot lunch table. It's like I'm some sort of food alien."

"Tell you what, let's go find something you can eat. Come with me." Mr. K motioned to the party parent in charge that he'd be right back and then led Randy out of the classroom.

On their way to the cafeteria, they passed a short woman with orange-red hair, yellow-green eye shadow, and miniature Christmas ornaments hanging from her ears. The name "Judy" was stitched on the pocket of her light blue shirt.

"Judy, we were just coming down to see you," Mr. K said. "I was hoping you might have a special gluten-free treat for Randy. He can't have the cookies the PTO provided for the party."

Judy squinted at Randy, smushing her wrinkled face. "I don't have anything in the kitchen, but the PTO brought in a special box of gluten-free cupcakes. Some of the teachers on staff are gluten-sensitive. I bet you can find an extra cupcake in the teacher's lounge."

Mr. K thanked her and headed down the hall, past the main office. He stopped in front of the teacher's lounge. Randy wasn't too excited about a gluten-free cupcake, but at least he'd get to see where all the teachers hung out. That was a bonus.

He waited for Mr. K to open the door and then

followed him inside. He took a step with his right foot, but before he could put his left foot down, his entire body floated up into the air like he had just bounced off a trampoline! Instead of coming back down, he stayed there, slowly rotating in place.

"What's happening?" He glanced around the white-walled cramped enclosure. Mr. K floated beside him, wearing a puffy white spacesuit. Randy looked down and gasped when he realized he was wearing one, too. "Whoa. Wait a minute. Are we in space? How did we get here? I'm pretty sure it wasn't in a rocket ship." He hoped they hadn't been abducted by aliens.

Mr. K somersaulted. "Welcome aboard the

International Space Station."

Randy grabbed onto a bar attached to the wall to keep himself upright. He studied Mr. K. "Yeah, right. This must be one of those places that lets you feel what it's like to be weightless. There's no way we're actually in outer space."

"Take a look outside that window over there and tell me what you see." Mr. K pointed toward a small round window divided into several triangle shapes.

Randy maneuvered along the wall until he reached the window. The view was so shocking, he let go of the wall, floated up, and bumped his head on the capsule's ceiling.

"That's insane," he whispered. "Is that Earth?"

A giant blue mound with swirls of white, brown, and green loomed in the distance, surrounded by a never-ending blanket of darkness.

Mr. K hovered beside Randy and nodded.

"If the Earth is round, why can't I see the bottom?" About halfway down, a wall of black seemed to cut the world in half.

"The sun's not shining on that part of the world right now, so it's nighttime down there."

"Are the white swirls supposed to be clouds?" "I believe so."

"And I'm guessing the dark splotches are land. It's so weird. From up here, you can see all the way to the oceans. But when you're on Earth, you can't see space. It's like a secret two-way mirror."

Mr. K and Randy bobbed in silence for several minutes.

"What exactly are we doing here?" Randy turned toward Mr. K. "I thought we were just going to get a crummy cupcake. Hey, did you win some teacher in space contest or something? Because that's cool if you did, but I'm pretty sure my mom will freak out if I'm not home in time for dinner."

Mr. K chuckled. "The astronauts on the space station live up here for months at a time. Sometimes there's only one of them. They stay in these tight living quarters and have to eat special food—dehydrated food that comes in little packets. I'm sure there are many days when they'd give anything for a nice juicy hamburger hot off the grill or a rich chocolate cupcake piled high with frosting."

"I know how they feel," Randy mumbled.

"Just think how lonely the astronauts must be at times. They don't get to hang out with their friends, sleep in their own beds, or feel the warmth of the sun on their faces during the day."

"Man, that sounds worse than having to sit alone at the peanut-free table. Remind me not to be an astronaut. Why would someone go through all that?"

"For the chance to get just one glimpse at that."

Mr. K nodded toward the triangular window.

Randy gazed back out into the universe. It truly

was the most awesome thing he'd ever seen. He could probably stare at it all day long.

"Sometimes you have to make sacrifices in order to get rewards," Mr. K said. "What happens when you eat foods with gluten or come in contact with peanuts?"

"Gluten makes me feel really sick, and peanuts can cause me to stop breathing."

"So don't you think it's worth eating gluten-free foods and sitting at the peanut-free table so you can feel good and be able to play sports and hang out with your friends?"

Randy cracked a smile. "Yeah, I guess it is. And I can see why the astronauts live all cooped up in here, too." He turned his attention back to the window.

"You want to go outside?"

Randy gave Mr. K a startled look. "What? You mean outside outside? Like go out into space?"

"We are dressed for it." Mr. K opened a cabinet door in the wall and removed two space helmets. He placed one over Randy's head and secured it in place. Then he put one on himself. He also attached two flexible tubes to the back of their suits.

"When I push this button, the room will depressurize and the hatch will open." His voice came through a speaker in Randy's helmet. "Just follow me out."

"If you say so." Randy's heart thumped, and

sweat dripped down his body inside the space suit.

Mr. K pressed a round red button on a control panel, and a loud whooshing sound filled the tiny room. Seconds later, part of the wall slid open, leading directly out into space. He bounded through the door and motioned for Randy to follow.

Randy took a few clumsy steps and then let his body float out of the space station. He moved quickly, and the long tube attached to his suit pulled him back when he floated too far; it reminded him of a dog being pulled back on its leash by its owner.

He gazed out into infinity, surprised at how much stuff there was in space—tiny particles that looked like flecks of colored dust, a few pieces of metal, and swirls of grey and white that danced in and out of flashes of twinkling stars. He floated toward the front of the space station and noticed someone watching them through the window—he could just make out the woman's orange-red hair. Wait a minute, was the lunch lady on the space station?

Randy was about to ask Mr. K when an especially bright dot of light caught Randy's eye. It looked almost blue, and it seemed to be growing brighter… and closer. It moved quickly, and then he noticed it was attached to something, like a headlight on a car.

"Uh, Mr. K? Is that a satellite orbiting Earth?"

Mr. K didn't respond. He stared in the direction of the light. Randy grabbed the safety tube and pulled himself toward the space station, trying to keep his distance from the strange object.

The light slowed down, and just when it looked like it might crash into the space station, it turned. That's when Randy realized it was a headlight, attached to a saucer-shaped spaceship. A clear dome covered the top, and staring at him and Mr. K through the glass was a green pointy head and two large black eyes. It raised a green, three-fingered hand and waved.

Stunned, Randy slowly waved back. In the next instant, the ship turned, and with a bright flash of blue light, it zipped away and disappeared into the darkness.

"Was that what I think it was?" Randy finally asked.

Mr. K floated over to him. "Did you really believe humans were the only ones living in this great big universe?" He patted Randy on top of his helmet. "Come on. The rest of the third-grade earthlings are waiting for us."

He pushed a button on the outside of the space station, opening the hatch. Randy pulled himself toward the door and climbed through—right back into his classroom. The space suit was gone, and his classmates were chatting in-between stuffing their faces with cookies and slurping on their juice pouches. Randy approached his seat and noticed something sitting on top of his tray table—a chocolate cupcake with blue frosting and white, brown, and green swirls. His very own Earth cupcake! Randy picked it up and grinned.

Mr. K walked up beside him. "It's gluten and peanut-free, and I guarantee it's out of this world." Then he smiled a half-smile.

5. THE REMARKABLE MASQUERADER

When the third-graders returned to school in January after the New Year, they couldn't hide their disappointment. The foot of snow they received had been great for sledding during winter break, but it meant cold, dreary winter days and indoor recess at school. It wasn't until February that they had something to look forward to— Valentine's Day. At least they'd get to restock their candy piles that had already dwindled from the holidays.

In art class, Mrs. White let the students decorate boxes for their Valentine cards. Sage cut and pasted red and pink construction paper hearts all over her white box and then sprinkled them with silver glitter. She wrote "SA" on one side of the card slit and "GE" on the other using a black marker.

"Sage, your Valentine box is positively radiant." Mrs. White clasped her hands in front of her mouth, admiring the project.

Sage smiled at her teacher but was distracted by Mrs. White's appearance. Her dark, chin-length hair had streaks of gray framing each side of her face, and her bangs feathered out like wings. She reminded Sage of a black and white bird.

After class, the students took their Valentine boxes back into their classroom. Sage set hers on the shelf below the window beside Randy's, whose box was covered in green and blue skulls and crossbones.

"I like your box."

"Thanks." Randy glanced at hers. "Yours isn't half bad, either."

"Did you buy your cards yet?" Sage asked.

"Yeah, I got outer space cards with alien tattoos. Fake ones. I mean, the tattoos are fake, not the aliens. Aliens are real."

Sage thought Randy's babbling was charming. "I

got my cards, too. I already have yours picked out. I think you'll really like it." She gave her best grin but clamped her mouth shut when she heard giggling behind her.

"I think someone likes you, Randy," Whitney said.

"Aww. The barbarian has a boyfriend." Woody snorted as he laughed.

Randy's face turned licorice-red. "We do not like each other. End of story."

Randy's words stung like a scraped knee. Sage snatched her Valentine box off the shelf, stormed toward the door, and threw the box in the trash can on her way out of the room. Outside in the hallway she leaned with her back against the wall and crossed her arms over her chest, pouting.

Mr. K stuck his head out of the doorway. When he saw Sage, he closed the door behind him and knelt down in front of her. "Anything I can do to help, besides giving Woody his own pop quiz?"

"I wish people noticed me for something other than how tall I am," Sage said.

"I know how you feel." Mr. K's warm eyes sparkled at her.

"I'm not small and cute like the other girls, and I'm taller and stronger than most of the boys. I can't win." Sage sniffed back her drippy nose.

Mr. K stood up. "What you need is a good ball. Come with me."

Sage frowned. The last thing she wanted to do was start crying in front of her teacher. She followed him down the hall and past the main office. He stopped in front of the teacher's lounge. If he thought she was going to have a pity party in the middle of the teacher's lounge, he was crazy.

Mr. K opened the door, and Sage tried to protest. "Mr. K, I'm fine, really. It's no big deal…" Her voice faded once she stepped inside—right into the most elaborate room she had ever seen.

Sage and Mr. K stood at the top of a grand, winding staircase that opened onto a black and white marble floor. Crystal chandeliers hung from the ornate domed ceiling. Round tables draped in white tablecloths lined the sides of the room with red velvet-cushioned chairs tucked around them. The center of the room housed clusters of dancers— men dressed in black formal wear and women gliding gracefully beside them, their floor-length, jewel-colored gowns twirling around their ankles.

As Sage looked closer, she noticed something strange about the dancers' faces; each one wore a mask that covered only their eyes. Most of the men wore plain black or white masks, but the women's were colorful, full of feathers, sequins, and glitter to match their fancy dresses.

Sage glanced up at Mr. K and gasped. He, too, wore a black tuxedo like the dancers, and his brown eyes peered at her through a black mask. That's when Sage looked down at herself. A gold satin dress billowed around her legs, the waist encrusted with shimmering crystals. Long, delicate gloves covered her arms to her elbows, and gold-colored ballet flats peeked out from under the hem of her skirt. She felt like Cinderella at a ball.

"Are we at a costume party?" she asked.

"It's a masquerade ball," Mr. K said. "So you'll need this." He held out a gold-colored eye mask with a crown of gold and silver-painted feathers around the top. Each eye hole was rimmed in clear crystals that matched the ones on her dress.

"Why do I need a mask? What are we doing

here?"

"You said you wanted to be noticed for something other than your height. Here, nobody will pay any attention to that. In fact, they don't even know who you are. This is your chance to let them see a different side of you."

Sage glanced at the dancers. "But who are all these people?"

"It's up to you to find out."

Sage took the mask from Mr. K and secured the thin elastic carefully around her hair. Mr. K offered her his arm, and she hooked hers through his elbow as he escorted her down the spiral staircase. He led her to the middle of the sea of dancers, turned to face her, gave a slight bow, and then disappeared into the crowd.

Flustered, Sage whirled around, searching for him, but all of the men looked the same. Dancers twirled in and around her to the beat of the waltz that the band played from the front of the room. A woman spun from the right and paused beside Sage. She wore a puffy white dress with a black satin sash and her white mask was covered in black feathers except for two white ones on either side. She looked just like a bird.

"Mrs. White?" Sage asked, but the woman spun away, back to her dance partner.

Sage felt dizzy and stumbled off the dance floor

toward one of the tables. She grabbed the back of a chair to steady herself and took a deep breath.

"Are you okay?"

Sage jumped at the voice and then turned to face a boy a few inches shorter than her dressed in a black suit and matching eye mask that had shimmering crystals surrounding the eye holes, just like hers.

"Yeah, I just got a little dizzy on the dance floor," she said.

"I couldn't help notice you out there," the boy said.

Sage was glad he couldn't see her disappointment behind her mask. Even in disguise she stood out like a weed in the middle of a flower garden.

"You have the best costume of anyone here," the boy said. "Did you make the mask yourself?"

Sage's eyelids fluttered. She stared at the boy and wished he'd take off his mask. She sensed she knew him but couldn't be sure.

"Um, no, I didn't make the mask. But thanks."

"So, do you wanna dance? I promise I won't twirl you around too much and get you dizzy."

Sage couldn't believe her luck. A boy wanted to dance...with her! "Yeah, sure. Okay." She followed him to a corner of the dance floor that wasn't so crowded. She stood still, her arms hanging at her sides, unsure what to do.

"This is a waltz. Follow the beat, one-two-three, one-two-three. And if that doesn't work, just shuffle your feet." He grinned, and Sage chuckled.

He clasped his left hand in her right hand and lightly placed his other hand at her waist. She tried to put her hand on his waist, but it collided with his arm, so she rested it on his shoulder instead.

The orchestra music filled the room, and Sage's tip-toe steps turned into long, graceful strides. She felt the three-step beat in the pit of her stomach and soon didn't have to think about her feet at all.

"You're a great dancer. What do you do besides waltz?" the boy asked.

"I play a lot of sports," Sage said.

"The only sport I play is tennis. And even then

I'm not very good. Half the time it winds up in the net."

"I love tennis. But I have the opposite problem. I hit it too hard and it goes out."

"We'd make a good team. I could play up close and get the short shots, and you could handle the long ones. We should play doubles sometime."

Sage was about to agree when someone ran into her, shoving her into her dance partner. Her face smashed against his jacket, and one of the gold feathers fell off her mask.

"Excuse you." A short, chubby boy glared at her through a crumpled black mask. He wore black-rimmed glasses over it and was dancing with a dainty girl in a purple satin dress.

"You ran into me," Sage said.

"How was I supposed to know there was a tree dancing beside me?" The boy cackled.

Sage turned away, ready to run for the door. This was exactly what she didn't want to happen. Even in disguise she stood out. She spotted Mr. K standing on the staircase. He shook his head. He didn't want her to run away from this.

She turned back around and faced the boy. "Leave us alone. We're just trying to dance."

"You call that dancing? Watch out, buddy. She'll bruise your feet," the short boy said.

"Knock it off," said Sage's dance partner.

"What, you're gonna let your boyfriend try to defend you?"

Anger knotted in Sage's chest and she grabbed her partner's hand and pulled him to the center of the marble dance floor. "Let's do this," she said.

The band struck up a faster song, and Sage danced around her partner. She held his hand and reached their arms above their heads. She spun in a circle first and then let him spin in a circle. He picked up on her rhythm. He let go of one of her hands and she twirled away, and then he pulled and she twirled back in. The crowd around them stopped dancing and circled around them, smiling in awe.

Sage continued to fast-step, twirl, and spin

as her partner led her around the dance floor. At the end of the song, he placed one hand behind her back and dipped her backward, supporting her in that final pose as the crowd clapped and cheered. Then he helped her stand up and they bowed. The short boy stormed off the floor. The dancers filled back in around them as a new song started up.

Sage's partner laughed. "That was incredible! I've never had so much fun. You can be my dance partner any time you want."

"I was just tired of people only noticing me for my height," Sage said.

"Well now people will know you as the most amazing dancer. And I'll know you as a good friend.

By the way, what's your name?"

Before Sage had a chance to answer, Mr. K appeared beside them.

"Pardon me, may I cut in?"

"I guess so," Sage said. She wasn't sure what the proper response was.

"I'll go get us some lemonade," her partner said.

"That was some fancy footwork out there," Mr. K said. "How did it feel?"

"It felt great. I could dance all night," Sage said. "I'm afraid it's time to go."

Sage wasn't ready. She was just starting to have fun. "But I didn't even get to tell him my name."

"I'm positive he'll never forget you," Mr. K said. He

offered Sage his arm and escorted her back up the staircase—and right into the hallway outside their classroom.

Sage hesitated at the door. "Nothing has changed. They'll still make fun of me."

"They might try, but they'll stop once you show them it doesn't bother you, just like you did at the ball."

Sage walked into the classroom and headed to her seat. Her tray table was down, and sitting on it was her Valentine box.

Randy came over when he saw her. "I hope it's okay. I got it out of the trash and glued the hearts back on that had fallen off."

"You did? Thanks."

"Aw, aren't the barbarian and her boyfriend cute?" Woody taunted from across the room.

"Hey, Woody. How about you and I arm wrestle and if I win, you have to stop calling me the barbarian," Sage called back to him. Her classmates cheered at the bet.

Woody looked flustered. "No way."

"What's the matter, Woody? Afraid you'd be beaten by a girl?" Eli teased.

"No. It wouldn't be fair. To Sage. No point in embarrassing her." Woody slumped down in his seat.

Sage grinned. She wondered if she was the only one who noticed that Woody had just called her by her real name.

"I have something I wanted to give you. I thought this might look good on your Valentine box." Randy held out a gold feather between his fingers.

Sage gasped. It was just like the feather that had fallen off her mask at the ball. "Where did you find this?"

"It just sort of...turned up," Randy said.

Sage glanced at Mr. K, who smiled a half-smile.

6. THE DEVOTED DOG HANDLER

The spring months brought many dreary days of rain, but one day in early April was gloomier than most. Eli was running late for school as usual. He raced down the stairs, rounded the corner in his living room, and skidded across the wood kitchen floor. He was about to grab his lunch bag when he noticed his dog lying by the back door. Instead of greeting Eli in the kitchen, Thor whimpered and swished his fluffy grey and white tail against the floor like a mop.

"What's the matter, boy?" Eli knelt down and rubbed Thor behind his ears. The dog whimpered again without lifting his head. "Mom, what's wrong with Thor?"

Mrs. Schultz knelt down beside him. "I'm afraid he hasn't been feeling well the last few days and is slowing down. The vet said his old age is catching up with him."

"Old age? But he's only twelve."

"That's pretty old for a dog. He's going to have to take it easy."

"Can't we give him some medicine or something to

make him feel better?" Eli stared into Thor's bright blue eyes.

"I'm afraid there's not much we can do for him except give him a lot of extra love."

Eli gasped and threw his arms around Thor's neck. "How can you say that? There's gotta be something we can do!" He buried his face in the dog's thick, warm fur.

"I didn't mean to upset you. We can talk about it after school. Thor will still be here when you get home." Eli's mom pried him off of Thor, wiped his face with a tissue, and helped him put on his tennis shoes. She kissed him on the forehead and drove him to school so he didn't have to walk in the rain.

Eli walked into his classroom in a daze. He couldn't imagine life without Thor. His dog had been with them as long as he could remember. Thor was like his best friend—always happy to see him and ready to play chase, tug of war, or ball at any moment. Thinking about losing Thor made Eli want to crawl under the covers and never come out.

During writing time, Mr. K had the students do a journal assignment. Eli wrote two whole pages about Thor. His eyes teared up again when he turned in the notebook.

"Eli, are you all right?" Mr. K asked.

"I wrote about my dog Thor." Eli swallowed hard. "He's old and not doing very good."

"I'm so sorry to hear that." Mr. K glanced at the paper. "I'm looking forward to reading about him."

"I don't want him to die," Eli blurted.

"Nobody does. It's so hard losing a pet."

"I wish there was some way to help him."

Mr. K stood up, pushing his chair back. "I think Mr. McCallister would be a good person to talk to about Thor. Come with me."

Eli rolled his eyes. He didn't need to talk to the school counselor. He needed to talk to someone who could help him save Thor.

He trudged down the hallway behind Mr. K, who stopped in front of the door marked "**COUNSELOR**" and knocked. The door opened and they were greeted by a man with shaggy gray hair whose white dress shirt stretched tight across his belly.

"Mr. McCallister, would you have time to talk with Eli? His dog is ill."

The counselor gave Eli a sympathetic smile. "I'd be happy to just as soon as I finish speaking with another student. Can you give me ten minutes?"

Eli could give him ten years. There wasn't anything this guy could say to make him feel better.

Mr. K nodded and glanced down at Eli. "You know, last spring I found a baby robin on the ground in my back yard. It had fallen out of a nest in the tree and injured its wing. I brought it indoors and took care of it for weeks. I even dug through the dirt in the garden to find fresh worms for it to eat." Mr. K grimaced.

Eli cracked a smile. He couldn't imagine a big guy like Mr. K digging for worms and feeding them by hand to a baby bird.

Mr. K slowly walked down the hall as he spoke. "I named the robin Little Red, and every time he saw me he chirped. He'd even sit on my shoulder while I read the newspaper. But once his wing healed, he started flying all over the house. I really wanted to keep him, but he needed more space. I knew it was time to let him go." Mr. K stopped in front of another door.

Eli read the "**TEACHER'S LOUNGE**" sign and gave Mr. K a confused look. "I don't get what all this has to do with Thor."

"You will." Mr. K opened the door and Eli 84 peered into the room. The few tables sat empty and he noticed a water cooler in one corner. He stepped inside and pulled the door shut behind him. When he turned back around, everything had changed.

The deserted room was now a crowd-filled arena. He stood at ground level overlooking a fancy, green-carpeted floor. For a second he thought they were at a concert. Then a dog's bark caught his attention. A parade of people with perfectly-groomed dogs marched onto the carpeted area and stopped in a single-file line. The dogs were all sizes and colors, heads held high and tails wagging.

"Uh, Mr. K? Are we at a dog show?" If watching a bunch of dogs prance around in a circle was supposed to make Eli feel better about Thor, it wasn't going to work.

"I don't want you to focus on the dogs, I want you to watch the handlers," Mr. K said.

"Isn't a dog show about the best-looking dog?" Eli asked.

"It's much more than that. A dog relies on its handler to give it clues what to do. The two have to work together and be in sync. The best looking dog in the world won't win if its handler doesn't guide it in the right direction."

Eli was still confused, but his thoughts were

interrupted when a man walked by with shaggy gray hair wearing a black tuxedo with the jacket pulled tight across his belly. He stood behind a podium at one end of the carpeted area. Eli could have sworn it was Mr. McCallister, but he couldn't quite tell from that far away.

Mr. K leaned over and whispered in Eli's ear. "That's the judge."

Behind Eli, high-pitched barking erupted in the arena. A tiny, hairless dog rocketed onto the carpet as a girl dressed in a T-shirt, jeans, and flip flops chased after it.

"Cupcake, no! Come back!" The girl's voice matched her horrified expression.

The rat-like dog ran in circles and then ran straight toward Eli. It darted in between his legs and stopped, cowering underneath him.

The girl jogged up to him, breathless, and snatched the dog's leash. "Oh, thank goodness. She may be small, but she's fast. I shouldn't have put her down after grooming, but I was trying to call her handler."

"What do you mean?" Mr. K asked.

"Her handler hasn't shown up yet, and Cupcake is supposed to be in this group." The girl nodded toward the dogs waiting in the arena. "I'd do it, but I'm not dressed for it." She pointed to her flip flops.

"You know, I think Eli here would make a good

handler," Mr. K said. "He has lots of experience with dogs."

Eli stared at his teacher in disbelief. "What? I don't know anything about showing dogs."

"It's not that hard. Just keep the leash tight so she stays right by your side. Don't let her get ahead of you or she'll look behind her to see where you're at. And be careful not to step on her. She's little." The girl handed Eli Cupcake's pink leash. "Good luck!"

Eli looked down at the scrawny tan dog. She must be some type of Chihuahua with her bug eyes and pointy ears. She wasn't soft and cuddly like Thor. But when he noticed her body shaking, he felt kind of sorry for her.

"The judge is waiting," Mr. K said. "You better take your place in line. Don't worry—just give Cupcake some encouragement, and she'll know what to do."

Eli sighed and wrapped the pink leash around his hand to make it shorter. He positioned Cupcake on his left side, which he knew was how dogs were supposed to heel, and started jogging toward one end of the arena. Half-way there he heard a small yelp and felt the dog's tiny foot underneath his own.

"Sorry," he mumbled. He had already stepped on the dog ten seconds into it. This was going to be a disaster.

He stopped next to a lady wearing a black skirt and jacket. Sitting perfectly still by her side was a Great Dane. Cupcake didn't even come up to its knee. The dog and its handler looked down their noses at Eli and Cupcake.

Eli ignored them and turned his attention back to the center of the arena where the first dog and handler in line took their lap. The small white dog pranced around the carpet, its feathery fur framing its proud face. The dog never looked up at its owner, who smiled as she jogged beside it.

One by one each competitor took a turn around the arena. Eli studied the handlers, hoping to pick up some tips, but it looked like all they did was just run the dogs in a circle. Except for the Great Dane. When it was his turn, he didn't wait for his handler. The muscular dog stepped out and took command like a war horse. His handler sprinted just to keep up, but she didn't need to be there at all. The Great Dane knew what he was doing.

Once they reached their place back in line with the other competitors, it was Eli's and Cupcake's turn. As they stepped out, the Great Dane let out a low growl. Cupcake jumped and froze in place, trembling.

Eli glared at the dog and his owner before bending down to stroke Cupcake's miniature back. "It's okay, girl. I won't let him hurt you. Let's go for our walk."

He wrapped her pink leash around his hand and gave it a little tug to get her going. Her short legs started up and she skittered across the green carpet. Even with her at full speed, Eli needed to keep his pace slow.

But adjusting his pace to hers was difficult. He slowed down, but she got ahead of him, forcing her to look up with a frightened expression to see where he was. Then she ran into his leg and he stepped on her paw— again.

Frustrated, he stopped mid-lap and waved at the judge. "Excuse me, sir? I'm new to this handler thing and am still getting used to it. Can I go back and start over?"

The gray-haired judged gave Eli a sympathetic smile and nodded.

Relieved, Eli scooped up Cupcake and ran back to his starting point. He needed to figure out a way to set a steady pace so she didn't run into him. That was his job as handler. He glanced at the Great Dane, who really was big enough to be a small horse. Wait...that was it. A horse!

Eli nuzzled Cupcake and whispered in her ear. "We're going to try something different." He set her down and tugged on her leash. She started running, her little legs moving like a hamster on a wheel. Then instead of walking or jogging, Eli started galloping—

like a horse.

Galloping allowed him to keep one foot directly in front of the other and in a straight line so he wouldn't step on Cupcake. He could gallop just fast enough to stay ahead of her but not so fast she couldn't keep up.

The little Chihuahua glanced at him only once and then seemed to pick up on his rhythm.

Several of the other handlers in line gasped and the audience pointed and laughed, but Cupcake kept trotting. Mr. K gave Eli a nodding approval as he galloped by. They completed their lap and returned to their place in line. The Great Dane let out another growl, but his handler shushed him and smiled at Eli.

The judge came out from behind his podium and the audience quieted down. He approached each dog, inspecting its head, coat, and tail. Cupcake held her head high during her inspection, and Eli held his breath, hoping his galloping wouldn't count against them. The judge looked a lot like Mr. McCallister.

The judge walked back and forth in front of the line of competitors twice, and then in one swift motion of his arm he pointed to three dogs—the Great Dane, the small, white long-haired dog, and Cupcake. The audience cheered, but Eli looked around, confused.

"What just happened?" he asked the Great Dane's handler.

"The judge picked first, second, and third place. Congratulations. You won third."

Eli stared at her in disbelief. Then he picked up Cupcake and kissed her on top of her head. "Did you hear that, girl? You won third place!" Cupcake licked Eli's chin as he made his way toward Mr. K and Cupcake's groomer.

"Wow, great job," the girl said. "I've never seen a handler gallop, but it really worked."

"I told you he knew a lot about dogs," Mr. K said.

"I just needed to find a pace that worked for her." Eli petted the top of Cupcake's silky head. "You know what? I think that's what I need to do for

Thor, too. He may be old and not able to play fetch anymore, but we could take little walks around the yard, and I can even build a ramp so he can get up on my bed at night." As if to agree, Cupcake let out a loud bark.

"I think she's hungry after all that exercise," the groomer said. "I'll take her in the back and feed her. Thanks again."

Eli gave Cupcake one more pat and then handed her to the groomer. He followed Mr. K through a door that led them out of the arena—back into the hallway at school right outside the counselor's office.

Mr. McCallister opened the door. "I'm ready for you now, Eli."

Eli stepped inside his office and noticed a photo of a tiny tan Chihuahua lying on Mr. McCallister's desk. "Is that your dog?"

"No, she's not mine. I help the Humane Society place foster dogs. The owner had to give her up and I'm trying to find her a good home. Know anyone who might be interested?"

"Yeah. I think I do." Eli glanced into the hallway at Mr. K, who smiled a half-smile.

7. THE INSIGHTFUL STUDENT-TEACHER

With only one week left of the school year, it was hard to believe summer was almost here. The third graders started cleaning out their seat pockets and taking home supplies. Even though Grayson finally agreed with Woody that Mr. K was the best teacher ever, he still didn't have any proof their teacher was magical. His classmates all had stories about the teacher's lounge, but Mr. K had never taken him in there. After a whole year at Coyote Run, he still felt like the new kid who was left out all the time.

On the second to the last day, Grayson walked into class and found out they had a sub—their first all year. Whitney, Woody, Eli, Sage, and Randy were huddled around Woody's seat.

"What's the deal with the sub? Where's Mr. K?" he asked.

"The bean's a little slow, better bring him up to speed," Woody said.

Grayson glared at him. He was the only one in class Woody still teased. Even Sage wasn't called the barbarian anymore.

Whitney gave Grayson an eager look. Ever since her appearance on "Brain Warriors," she was the go-to person for all information. "I overheard the sub talking to Principal Kohn when I walked in. He said Mr. K had a baby."

Woody snickered and Whitney gave him an annoyed look.

"Mr. K's wife had a baby. Last night."

"I didn't even know Mr. K was married," Randy said. "If Mrs. K is even half as tall as Mr. K, then that will be the tallest baby in history."

"When is he coming back?" Grayson asked.

"I don't think he is. It sounds like he's starting summer vacation early," Sage said.

The words shocked Grayson. Not coming back? How could Mr. K just ditch them at the end of the year? He had hoped Mr. K was saving his adventure for last, and if he had a cool story like everyone else, then Woody would finally consider him to be part of the group. Now it looked like that would never happen.

The bell rang and Grayson slumped into his seat. The sub, who looked a hundred years old with her floral dress, black clunky shoes, and hair pulled back in a bun, stood by the teacher's desk with her hands clasped in front of her. She glanced around the room and shook her head when she looked up at the JumboTron. Then she clapped three times for attention.

"Boys and girls, I am Mrs. Vermoss. I will be your teacher for the next two days while Mr. K is at home with his new baby—a girl, I believe. Principal Kohn printed out an email Mr. K sent, and I am to read it to you.

"Dear class, I am sorry for my unexpected absence, however, you will be in very good hands. Even though I am not there, the same rules still apply, and I will know if you follow them. I wouldn't feel right letting the school year end without saying goodbye, so I promise to stop up and see you all on the last day. Sincerely, Mr. K."

Grayson sighed. Maybe Mr. K was coming back

to do something really cool for them on the last day. The thought got him through the rest of the morning with Mrs. Vermoss, who spent most of her time walking up and down the rows insisting everyone straighten their seat backs and muttering how teaching just wasn't what it used to be.

During lunch recess, the class gathered on the blacktop by the basketball hoops. Whitney was on a mission to convince everyone they needed to write Mr. K thank you letters for being a good teacher.

"That sounds like an assignment," Woody complained. "It's the last week of school. We don't need more work."

"Why don't we just make him a card and have

everyone sign it?" Sage suggested.

"That doesn't seem special enough," Whitney said.

"We could throw him a popcorn party," said Randy. "That way we could eat it, too."

"What about getting him a gift? Maybe like a pet hamster to keep in the classroom that would remind him of us," said Eli, grinning.

Grayson didn't like any of those suggestions. "How about a baby gift? He did just have a baby."

Whitney squealed with excitement. "Yes! We could throw him a baby shower!"

"I don't think babies take showers," Woody said with a straight face.

"No, a baby shower is a party where you shower the parents with gifts for the baby. We could have it when he comes up to school on the last day. We could each get a small baby gift, decorate with pink and white balloons, and I could make cupcakes with pink and white frosting!"

Grayson wasn't sure how his gift suggestion had turned into an entire baby shower. If they took up all of Mr. K's time with the party, then there was no way anything else...special could happen.

"If we decorate the classroom, Mr. K will see it before he even walks in," Woody said. "If we want to really surprise him, we need to make it a total secret."

The word "secret" gave Grayson an idea. "Maybe we could have the party in the teacher's lounge. Mr. K would never suspect it there." It was his last chance to get into the teacher's lounge.

"Boy, the bean is full of good ideas today," Woody said.

"I'll ask Principal Kohn after school," Whitney said. "This will be the best surprise ever!"

Principal Kohn gave the third graders permission to use the teacher's lounge for Mr. K's baby shower, and Whitney instructed everyone to come to school early the next day to decorate and for everyone to bring a small gift.

Grayson's mom dragged him to the store after

school, forcing him to pick out baby clothes. "Why can't we just wrap up some of Janie and Jennie's old baby clothes? They have hundreds of them, and some still have the tags on." After Grayson's twin sisters were born, they were flooded with girly baby clothes—they got two of everything.

"It's important this gift comes from you." His mom held out two sleeper sacks. "These are so great, they're like pajamas and a blanket in one. Now, which one do you like, the pink bunnies or the yellow ducks?"

Grayson couldn't imagine Mr. K caring about bunnies or ducks. It seemed silly to buy a big guy like Mr. K teeny tiny baby clothes, especially ones that looked like bags. He wanted to get him something better—something that would make Mr. K remember him. But Grayson couldn't think what that might be, so instead he pointed to the sleeper sack with the bunnies.

On the last day of school, Grayson met the rest of his class in the teacher's lounge. He was surprised how ordinary the room seemed. All the tables were pushed together in the middle of the room, and a bouquet of pink and white balloons sat in the center. Surrounding it was a pile of pink gift bags and wrapped presents. A tray of bright-pink frosted cupcakes sat on the counter beside the fridge. Sage stood on a chair while Woody and Eli handed her pink and white streamers to hang from the ceiling. It was a good thing they had someone that tall in their class who could reach it.

Whitney glanced at Grayson. "Gifts go on the table. Then grab a chair and help Randy hang streamers on the other side of the room. Principal Kohn said Mr. K will be here at eight o'clock, and he'll bring him right to the teacher's lounge, so we need to be ready."

Grayson added his gift to the pile and helped Randy and Sage with a roll of streamers. They had barely finished when Principal Kohn stuck his head in to say Mr. K had arrived.

"Quick! Everyone gather in front of the table."

Whitney positioned them in place.

Grayson watched the door slowly open. This was it. What he had heard about all year. Mr. K and the teacher's lounge equaled magic.

The door opened to reveal Mr. K, holding a baby carrier.

"Surprise!" Whitney yelled louder than the rest.

Mr. K's mouth dropped open and his eyes twinkled as he glanced around the room. "It certainly is a surprise. Thank you. I wasn't expecting this when I walked in." He set the carrier on the table and Whitney and Sage stuck their faces in front of it to coo at the baby.

"Class, meet Baby K."

Grayson couldn't hide his disappointment that nothing had happened. He should have known. He was right from day one. Nothing magical about it. He stood on tiptoe to get a glimpse of the sleeping, bald- headed baby. She looked just like Mr. K.

"We got her presents," Whitney said. "After you open them, we can have cupcakes."

Mr. K sat down and the students gathered around him. He picked a gift bag out of the pile. Grayson groaned when he saw it was his. He was sure it would end up being the lamest gift.

Mr. K carefully unwrapped the tissue. He held up the bunny sleeper for everyone to see. "Oh, look at the cute dress."

Grayson's face felt warm from embarrassment.

"It's a sleeper sack—pajamas and a blanket in one. It's supposed to be good for babies, at least that's what my mom says, and she knows all about it from having my twin sisters."

Mr. K gave him an appreciative look. "Wow. I had no idea about this kind of thing. Thank you, Grayson. Being a new parent is a little overwhelming. It reminds me of my first day as a new teacher."

Grayson knew how hard it was to be new, but he couldn't believe Mr. K would have trouble with anything. "Parenting should be easy. You take care of twenty kids every day."

"I don't take care of you, I teach you. And you're

not little kids. I don't know the first thing about babies. I was supposed to give Baby K a bath this morning, but I was too nervous."

Grayson laughed. "Babies are easy. My dad says they're just like taking care of a car. Keep them full of gasoline, change the oil, wash the grime off them, and give them a lot of TLC. They'll last forever."

"Good one, bean." Woody chuckled.

"And my mom used to give my sisters baths in the kitchen sink. I can give you a bunch of other pointers, if you want," Grayson added.

"I would really like that. Baby K and I appreciate the help."

Grayson wasn't so embarrassed about his gift

anymore, especially after Mr. K opened up several packages of burp cloths, onesies, and bottles.

After gifts, Whitney passed around the tray of cupcakes. Grayson chose the cupcake with the thickest pile of pink frosting swirled on top and licked the wrapper clean.

Mr. K stood from the table and grabbed the baby carrier. "Thank you again for the wonderful party and gifts. You had better get to class. Mrs. Vermoss will be waiting. Woody, Eli, Randy, Whitney, and Sage— would you mind staying just for a minute?"

Grayson lingered at the table while the rest of the students told Mr. K goodbye on their way out of the teacher's lounge. Why hadn't Mr. K asked him to stay? Was this some sort of teacher's lounge club and he wasn't allowed? Angry and confused, he stomped toward the door.

"Oh, Grayson, would you stay as well?" Mr. K asked.

At the sound of his teacher's voice, Grayson froze, smiling. Maybe he wouldn't be left out, after all. He spun around, expecting to join his classmates. Instead, the roar of engines and a blast of air from a speeding car nearly knocked him down. He looked out onto an oval race track. Mr. K and his classmates stood off to the side, all wearing matching blue and white jump suits. Mr. K held the baby in his arms—even she wore one.

"How did we...where are...what's going on?" Grayson sputtered.

"What you said about babies being like cars made a lot of sense," Mr. K said. "So I thought learning to drive a race car would be good practice for me. But I need someone to help me out. Care to ride along?"

A sleek race car with blue and white stripes pulled up beside them. The number "99" was painted on the side with the name "Coyote Run" below it. A woman wearing a floral jumpsuit and clunky black shoes stepped out of the car.

"Mrs. Vermoss?" Grayson whispered. He couldn't tell if it was her through her helmet. She took the baby out of Mr. K's arms. Grayson glanced at the other third-graders, who smiled back at him.

"They'll be our pit crew," Mr. K said. "It takes a lot of hands to make this baby run." He handed Grayson a helmet and then put one on himself.

Woody gave him a thumbs-up. "Go for it, Gray."

Grayson returned the gesture to his friend.

Mr. K walked around to the driver's side and Grayson slid into the passenger's seat. When Mr. K started the engine, it sent a rush of excitement through Grayson. He wondered if he was dreaming.

"Mr. K, thanks for deciding to include me. I don't feel like the new kid anymore."

"It's you I have to thank, Grayson. Sometimes I forget I can learn just as much from my students as they can learn from me. That's the real magic in teaching." Mr. K revved the engine, shifted the car into gear, and peeled out onto the race track, smiling a full smile.

About the Author

Kathy Sattem Rygg is the author of *The Crystal Cache* series as well as the author of the Hidden Gem award winning chapter books *Tall Tales with Mr. K* and *TALLER Tales with Mr. K*, and the author of the highly acclaimed middle grade book *Animal Andy*. She has more than 15 years of experience in marketing and public relations, and has held editorial positions for a number of publications. Ms. Rygg is from Omaha, NE, where she lives with her two children and enjoys sharing her love for writing.

About Us:

Knowonder is a leading publisher of engaging, daily content that drives literacy; the most important factor in a child's success.

Parents and educators use Knowonder tools and content to promote reading, creativity, and thinking skills in children from zero to twelve.

Knowonder delivers original, compelling new stories, creating an opportunity for parents to connect to their children in ways that significantly improve their children's success.

Ultimately, Knowonder's mission is to eradicate illiteracy and improve education success through content that is affordable, accessible, and effective.

About DyslexiAssist

The Font: When reading with this new font, independent research shows that 84% of dyslexics read faster, 77% read with fewer mistakes.

The Layout: But the magic isn't just in the font. The layout of the book is critical. In fact, recent peer-reviewed scientific research showed that all the dyslexic children read easier and faster with the proper increased spacing.

> Learn more, including how you can use DyslexiAssist in your home or classroom for FREE at knowonder.com/dyslexiassist

We'll show you the independent research, but even more importantlly, we'll teach you how to use the font and how to duplicate our layout. so you can use it in your home or classroom.

CPSIA information can be obtained
at www.ICGtesting.com
Printed in the USA
LVHW111255230119
604950LV00001B/29/P